Leonard Bernstein

(1918 – 1990)

Bernstein
for
Bassoon and Piano

Selected and Arranged by David J. Elliot

Photography by David Gahr

LEONARD
BERNSTEIN
Music Publishing
Company LLC

BOOSEY & HAWKES

CONTENTS

preface by the arranger

This collection of works for bassoon and piano has been selected and arranged to provide a wide variety of musical challenges for advanced student performers based on the rich musical legacy of one of America's greatest composers – Leonard Bernstein. In addition to such popular pieces as "MARIA" and "TONIGHT" from WEST SIDE STORY, this collection includes several equally beautiful but less familiar compositions from Bernstein's CANDIDE, MASS, ON THE TOWN, A QUIET PLACE, and CHICHESTER PSALMS.

In preparing and practicing your interpretations, it is important to keep in mind the original context of each piece. Berstein composed each of these works to be sung to a specific text and to occur at a particular point in the dramatic action or narrative of a larger musical work (e.g. a Broadway show, a mass.) Also, Bernstein's expressive instructions, dynamics, accents, tempi, etc., can be a further aid in the artistic interpretation and performance of each piece.

Every effort has been made to preserve the original keys and structures of these pieces and to include all the essential details of Bernstein's original orchestrations in the piano accompaniments. Sometimes, however, changes have been required to meet the particular demands of the bassoon and the piano.

David J. Elliot
1996

This collection was first published in 1997.

Vorwort des Arrangeurs

Diese Sammlung von Arbeiten für Fagott und Klavier wurde ausgewählt und bearbeitet, um den fortgeschrittenen, öffentlich auftretenden Musikstudenten auf der Basis des reichen Erbes eines der größten Komponisten Amerikas - nämlich Leonard Bersteins - eine große Vielfalt musikalischer Herausforderungen anhand zu geben. Zusätzlich zu solch populären Stücken wie „MARIA" und „TONIGHT" aus der WEST SIDE STORY enthält diese Sammlung mehrere ebenso schöne, aber weniger bekannte Kompositionen aus Bersteins CANDIDE, MASS, ON THE TOWN, A QUIET PLACE und CHICHESTER PSALMS.

Wenn Sie Ihre Interpretation vorbereiten und üben, ist es wichtig, daß Sie sich stets den ursprünglichen Zusammenhang eines jeden Stückes vor Augen halten. Berstein komponierte eine jede dieser Arbeiten, um zu einem bestimmten Text gesungen zu werden und an einer bestimmten Stelle innerhalb der dramatischen Handlung oder Geschichte einer größeren musikalischen Arbeit (z. B. einer Broadway Show, einer Messe) zu erscheinen. Bernsteins klare Anleitungen, seine Dynamik, Akzente, Tempi, etc. können außerdem weitere Hilfsmittel für die künstlerische Interpretation und Aufführung eines jeden Stückes sein.

Es wurde jede Bemühung unternommen, die Originaltonarten- und strukturen dieser Stücke beizubehalten und alle die wesentlichen Details von Bernsteins Originalorchestrierung in die Pianobegleitung zu integrieren. Gelegentlich jedoch waren Änderungen nötig, um den besonderen Anforderungen der Fagott und des Pianos nachzukommen.

David J. Elliott
1996

préface de l'arrangeur

Cette collection d'oeuvres pour basson et piano a été choisie et arrangée de manière à offrir, aux étudiants de niveau avancé, un vaste éventail de défis musicaux basés sur le riche legs musical de l'un des plus grands compositeurs américains : Leonard Bernstein. Outre les pièces bien connues telles que « MARIA » et « TONIGHT » tirées de WEST SIDE STORY, cette collection comprend plusieurs compositions tout aussi belles mais moins connues tirées des oeuvres suivantes de Bernstein : CANDIDE, MASS, ON THE TOWN, A QUIET PLACE et CHICHESTER PSALMS.

En préparant et pratiquant vos interprétations, il importe de garder en mémoire le contexte de chaque pièce à l'origine. Bernstein a composé chacune de ces oeuvres de manière à être chantée sur un texte particulier et à s'insérer à un moment précis de l'action dramatique ou de la narration d'une oeuvre musicale plus étendue (une messe ou une comédie musicale de Broadway, par exemple). En outre, les tempi, les accents, la dynamique, les instructions expressives de Bernstein peuvent aider également à l'interprétation artistique et à l'exécution de chaque pièce.

On n'a ménagé aucun effort pour préserver les clefs et les structures originales de ces pièces et pour inclure tous les détails essentiels des orchestrations initiales de Bernstein dans les accompagnements de piano. Certaines modifications ont, toutefois, dû être apportées en vue de satisfaire aux exigences particulières de la basson et du piano.

David J. Elliott
1996

prefacio del adaptador

Esta colección de obras para fagot y piano ha sido seleccionada y adaptada con el fin de proporcionar una amplia variedad de retos musicales a los intérpretes que sean estudiantes avanzados, basándose en el rico legado musical de uno de los más grandes compositores norteamericanos: Leonard Bernstein. Además de piezas tan populares como «MARIA» y «TONIGHT» de WEST SIDE STORY, en esta colección se incluyen varias composiciones igualmente hermosas, aunque menos conocidas, de las obras CANDIDE, MASS, ON THE TOWN, A QUIET PLACE y CHICHESTER PSALMS de Bernstein.

Para preparar y ensayar estas interpretaciones es importante considerar el contexto original de cada una de las piezas. Bernstein compuso todas estas obras para que fueran cantadas siguiendo un texto específico y para que tuvieran lugar en un punto concreto dentro de una acción o narración dramática de una obra musical más amplia (p. ej. un espectáculo de Broadway o una misa). Por otra parte, las instrucciones, la dinámica, los acentos y el tempo tan expresivos de Bernstein pueden ayudar todavía más en la interpretación artística y ejecución de cada una de estas piezas.

Se ha hecho todo lo posible por conservar el tono y la estructura original de las piezas musicales e incluir todos los detalles esenciales de las orquestaciones originales de Bernstein en los acompañamientos de piano. No obstante, algunas veces ha sido necesario realizar cambios para satisfacer las demandas particulares el fagot y el piano.

David J. Elliot
1996

MARIA
from WEST SIDE STORY

Bassoon

Music by
LEONARD BERNSTEIN

Bassoon

TONIGHT
from WEST SIDE STORY

Bassoon

SOMEWHERE
from WEST SIDE STORY

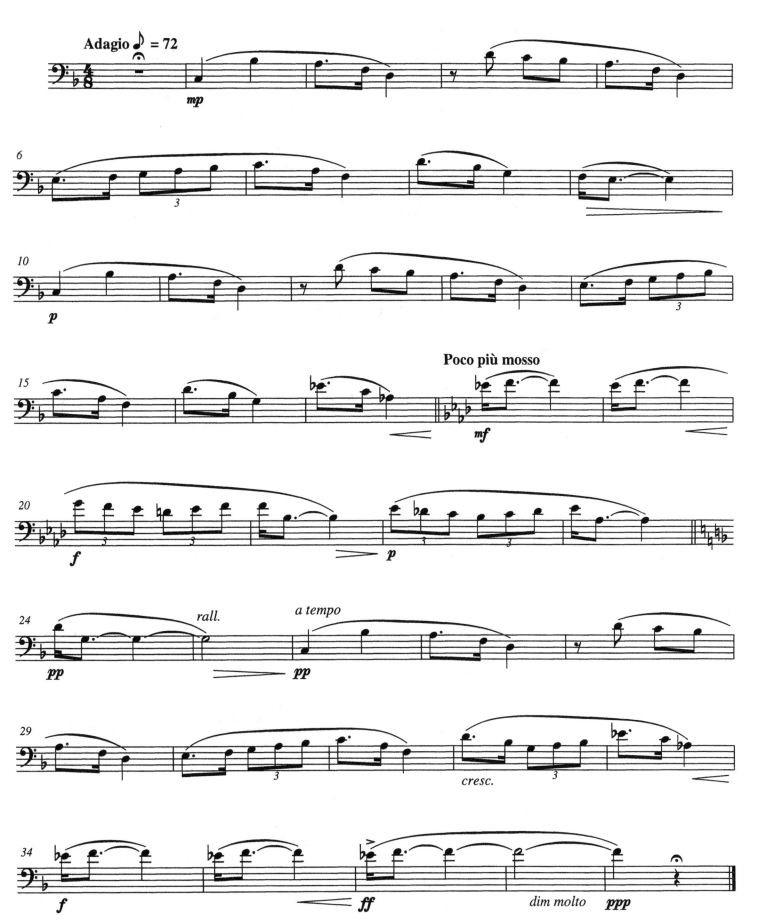

Bassoon

PSALM 23

2nd Movement from CHICHESTER PSALMS

Leonard Bernstein

(1918 – 1990)

Bernstein
for
Bassoon and Piano

Selected and Arranged by David J. Elliot

Photography by David Gahr

LEONARD
BERNSTEIN
Music Publishing
Company LLC

BOOSEY & HAWKES

CONTENTS

MARIA
from WEST SIDE STORY

Bassoon/Keyboard

Music by
LEONARD BERNSTEIN

Slowly and freely

Bassoon/Keyboard

TONIGHT
from WEST SIDE STORY

SOMEWHERE
from WEST SIDE STORY

Bassoon/Keyboard

PSALM 23
2nd Movement from CHICHESTER PSALMS

Bassoon/Keyboard

A SIMPLE SONG
from MASS

Bassoon/Keyboard

THERE IS A GARDEN
from TROUBLE IN TAHITI

LUCKY TO BE ME
from ON THE TOWN

Bassoon/Keyboard

I CAN COOK TOO

from ON THE TOWN

Bassoon/Keyboard

Tempo primo

Bassoon/Keyboard

OH, HAPPY WE
from CANDIDE

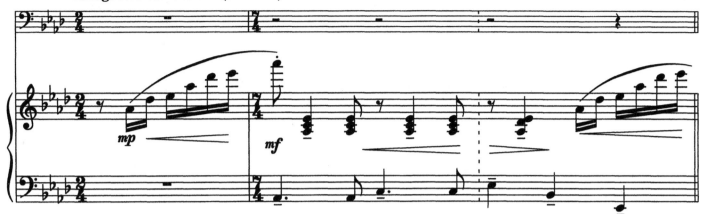

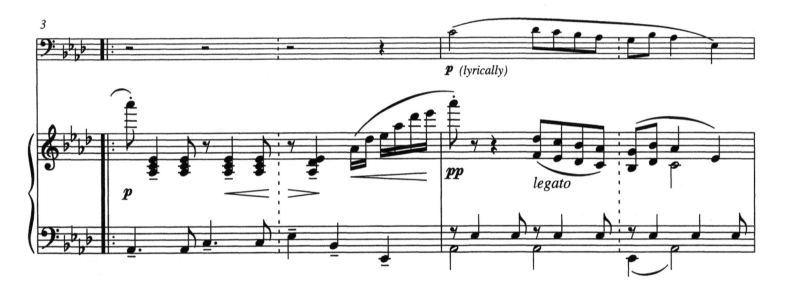

ONE HAND, ONE HEART
from WEST SIDE STORY

Bassoon/Keyboard

SOMETHING'S COMING
from WEST SIDE STORY

41

Bassoon/Keyboard

Bassoon

A SIMPLE SONG
from MASS

THERE IS A GARDEN

from TROUBLE IN TAHITI

LUCKY TO BE ME

from ON THE TOWN

Bassoon

I CAN COOK TOO

from ON THE TOWN

OH, HAPPY WE
from CANDIDE

Bassoon

ONE HAND, ONE HEART
from WEST SIDE STORY

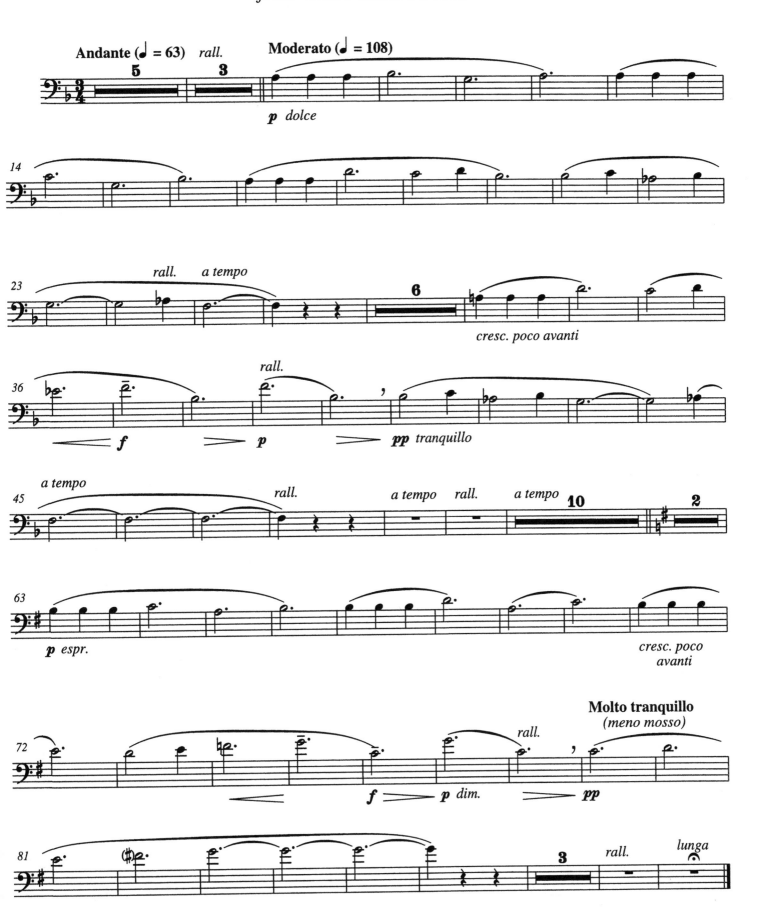

SOMETHING'S COMING
from WEST SIDE STORY